ELVIS SPEAKS

Other Books by Elizabeth McKeon and Linda Everett

The American Diner Cookbook:
More Than 450 Recipes and Nostalgia Galore

Cinema Under the Stars:
America's Live Affair with Drive-In Movie Theaters

Other Cumberland House Books About Elvis Presley

The Presley Family & Friends Cookbook

ELVIS SPEAKS

Thoughts on Fame, Family, Music, and More in His Own Words

Elizabeth McKeon
and
Linda Everett

CUMBERLAND HOUSE
NASHVILLE, TENNESSEE

ELVIS SPEAKS
CUMBERLAND HOUSE PUBLISHING, INC.
431 Harding Industrial Drive
Nashville, Tennessee 37211

Formerly published as *The Quotable King*.

Cover design by James Duncan Creative, Nashville, Tennessee

Library of Congress Cataloging-in-Publication Data

   Elvis speaks : thoughts on fame, family, music, and more in his own words / Elizabeth McKeon and Linda Evertt.
      p.   cm.
   Includes bibliographical references.
   ISBN 1-58182-394-0 (hardcover : alk. paper)
   1. Presley, Elvis, 1935–1977—Quotations. I. McKeon, Elizabeth, 1962– . II. Everett, Linda, 1946– .
ML420.P96E448 2004
782.42166'092—dc22   2004002973

To
Elvis fans everywhere
who keep
the memory of
his words and music
alive

CONTENTS

ACKNOWLEDGMENTS

A special thanks goes out to all our family and friends who helped and supported our efforts in putting this book together.

A special thanks to Ron and Julie Pitkin at Cumberland House for all their support and guidance.

Waiting outside the studio before going on the Frank Sinatra "Welcome Home, Elvis" special (Fontainbleu Hotel, Miami Beach, Florida, 1960)

INTRODUCTION

Elvis spoke to a whole generation of people through his music.

In songs such as "Heartbreak Hotel," Elvis conveyed the life of loneliness and heartache or the fate of romance in "Return to Sender."

Whether it was a ballad, a gospel hymn, or pure rock 'n' roll, when Elvis spoke, people listened.

But there was more to this man than lyrics to a song or a Hollywood script. Elvis was a thoughtful and polite man with his own visions, ideals, and opinions.

Away from the stage and the lights of a Hollywood set, Elvis could be found in the spotlight of the media.

In his early career he was constantly questioned about his "vulgar" and "sinful" stage act. He was forced to defend himself and his particular style of rocking to the musical beat. He spoke against the media's criticisms with thoughtful replies that he wasn't a "sex maniac" nor was he going against "God and his faith."

INTRODUCTION

Repeatedly he was asked personal questions ranging from love and marriage to his religious beliefs. Elvis wasn't the type to lord over his views and opinions on others, but when asked a question he answered it, always in a thoughtful, truthful way.

Being the shy, soft-spoken man that he was, Elvis stood by the values and morals he was raised to believe.

Elvis's untimely death at the age of forty-two left a void in the hearts of many who truly appreciated this man's talents. But Elvis will always be remembered and live on in our hearts through his recorded music and films, and most importantly through the words he spoke from his heart.

Elvis Speaks is a collection of Elvis's words—of what Elvis said on topics ranging from how he felt about being drafted into the army, his fans, performing in front of a live audience, to loneliness.

Elvis's words come from the heart and tell about the man beyond the entertainer, beyond the gates of Graceland, beyond the Cadillacs, and beyond the gold records and money.

Elvis Speaks is pure Elvis because the words are Elvis's and tell of a man who simply loved to entertain people and found heartache and happiness in a career that spanned nearly three decades.

ELVIS SPEAKS

Lauderdale Courts, Memphis, 1949

EARLY ELVIS

Elvis Presley grew up poor in the small Mississippi town of Tupelo, the only child of Gladys and Vernon Presley. Elvis was instilled with high moral values and a strong religious upbringing. As a young boy, Elvis was shy, polite, and always well-mannered.

While still in his early teens, Elvis and his family moved to Memphis, Tennessee, with the hope of a better future. While attending Humes High School in Memphis, Elvis had a close group of friends. He also worked at odd jobs to help support the family. His interest in music was evident as he sang in the choir when he attended church services.

One day, on a whim, Elvis decided to give his mother a recording of his voice singing a song for a birthday gift. The decision to record that song at Sun Records helped to launch Elvis's career as one of the greatest entertainers of the twentieth century.

"I always remember that I had a peanut in my mouth when that photo was taken."

—*Referring to the famous photo of him as a little boy*

"All my life I've always had a nice time. We never had any money or nothing, but I've always managed to. . . . I never had any luxuries, but we always . . . we never went hungry, you know. That's something to be thankful for, even if you don't have all the luxuries, because there's so many people who don't."

"I was raised in a pretty decent home and everything. My folks always made me behave, whether I wanted to or not."

"My mother always taught me to behave, to have good manners, to help people, not harm them, to work hard and never give up, and to make it on my own."

"I would lie awake wondering what I was going to do. I really wasn't much good at anything. At school I'd been only an average student. I mean I didn't flunk, but I didn't do too good, either. I couldn't figure out how I was ever going to make something out of myself."

"I'm so nervous. I've always been nervous, ever since I was a kid."

—*Why Elvis bit his nails*

Talking to fans outside the ranch-style home he bought for his parents on Audubon Drive in Memphis (1956)

"Mama worried that I wasn't taking care of myself."

☆ ☆ ☆

"My mama never let me out of her sight. I couldn't go down to the creek with the other kids."

"My mother—I suppose since I was an only child, we might have been a little closer—I mean everyone loves their mother, but I was an only child and mother was always right with me all my life. It wasn't only like losing a mother, it was like losing a friend, a companion, someone to talk to. I could wake her up any hour of the night, and if I was worried or troubled about something, she'd get up and try to help me. I used to get very angry at her when I was growing up. It's natural when a young person wants to go somewhere or do something and your mother won't let you—to think, 'why, what's wrong with you?' But later on in the years, you know, you find out that she was right. That she was only doing it to protect you and keep you from getting in any trouble and from getting hurt. And I'm very happy that she was kinda strict on me, very happy that it worked out the way it did."

ELVIS SPEAKS

10

"I always felt that someday, somehow, something would happen to change everything for me, and I'd daydream about how it would be."

"I always had to be polite and do the right things. My folks were real strict. I rebelled sometimes, but I guess their strictness was the best thing that ever happened to me, even if I didn't realize it. My Mom and Dad loved me too much ever to spoil me, even though I was an only child."

"I couldn't even go down to the creek with the other kids and swim. That's why I'm no swimmer today."

☆ ☆ ☆

"My Daddy never made much money, but I don't remember ever wanting something real bad that he wouldn't try to get it for me."

The famous profile once compared to John Barrymore's

"Mama never could do enough for me. She took me to all those church meetings every Sunday to make sure I didn't ever go wrong."

"The gospel is really what we grew up with more than anything else. It's just part of you, if you think about it."

"We were always happy as long as we were together."

—*Elvis and his parents*

☆ ☆ ☆

"We were broke man, broke . . . and we left for Memphis overnight."

Giving the camera his James Dean look on the patio at his Audubon Drive house (1956)

"We weren't the only family who was thankful to have a Christmas basket of groceries."

"I'd like to have gone, but I never thought about it. We just didn't have the money."

—Talking about why he never went to college

"We had nothing before, nothing but a hard way to go."

☆ ☆ ☆

"I know what poverty is. I lived it for a long time. . . . I am not ashamed of my background."

Another candid interview (left, 1956) and visiting a Memphis radio station for a chat (right, 1956)

Cruisin' down Memphis's Main Street (1956)

"I was a nobody, a small town kid in a big city, without a dime in my pocket, not too good in class, kinda shy . . . and the other guys wore GI haircuts. I wanted to look older, be different. I guess mostly I wanted to be noticed. My hair, the black shirt and pants I wore did it. But don't think I didn't take a lot of kidding from my friends. Still, I stuck with it. I guess I always knew if you want to stand out in a crowd you gotta be different."

"Wild-looking guys, they had scars. I used to lay on the side of the road and watch [them] drive their big diesel trucks."

—*Referring to truck drivers and the influence they had on his style*

"It was just something I wanted to do. I wasn't trying to be better than anybody else."

—Explaining why he liked to wear a different style of clothing

"How I happened to wear sideburns was, my Dad was a truck driver and I admired him and other truck drivers I knew. Most wore sideburns and mustaches. So when I was sixteen, I grew sideburns to look as much like them as possible."

Question: "Were you popular when you went to
school?"

Elvis: "Not too. I wasn't the big hero."

"I wasn't popular in high school. I wasn't dating
anybody [there]. I failed music—only thing I ever
failed. And then they entered me in this talent show
and I came out and did my first number, 'Til I Waltz
Again with You,' by Teresa Brewer. And when I came on
stage I heard people kinda rumbling and whispering
and so forth, 'cause nobody knew I even sang. It was
amazing how popular I became after that."

"I've never been accustomed to things real easy. I know it looks like I came up overnight. Not so! I can tell you that it was a lot of hard work. I've done plenty of it. I worked as a common laborer. I drove a truck for Crown Electrics in Memphis at the same time I was going to high school. I'd get up at 3:30 and be on the job at 6:30 for $12.50 a week. Luckily I don't need much sleep. I've got plenty of nervous energy."

In Memphis, posing with Dewey Phillips of WHBQ, the first DJ to play an Elvis record (1956)

Elvis: "If you know anyone that needs a singer . . ."

Marion : "What kind of singer are you?"

Elvis: "I sing all kinds."

Marion: "Who do you sound like?"

Elvis: "I don't sound like nobody."

Marion : "What do you sing—hillbilly?"

Elvis: "I sing hillbilly."

Marion : "Well who do you sound like in hillbilly?"

Elvis: "I don't sound like nobody."

—*Speaking for the first time to Marion Keisker at Sun Records*

"My daddy had seen a lot of people who played the guitar and stuff and didn't work, so he said: 'You should make up your mind either about being an electrician or playing a guitar. I never saw a guitar player worth a damn."

—*Vernon's feelings toward Elvis quitting his job*

"I never took any singing lessons and the only practicing I ever did was on a broom stick before my dad gave me my first guitar."

Outside Jim's barbershop in Memphis (1956)

"I'd really wanted to hear myself sing. I can't remember exactly what hit me that day, but I had to know what my voice sounded like."

> —*Talking about wanting to make a record for his mother's thirty-sixth birthday*

"I didn't have enough money to do the record over, so I decided to let it stand as it was. I figured if nobody else liked the thing, Mom would, anyway, and she did."

> —*Referring to the record Elvis made for his mom that launched his career*

"I guess I must've sat there at least three hours. I sang everything I knew—pop stuff, spirituals, just a few words of anything I remembered. I was an overnight sensation. A year after they heard me the first time, they called me back!"

"I ad lib everything. I never had a rehearsal in my life. When I recorded 'Blue Moon of Kentucky,' I didn't even know the words of it."

—Talking about learning to read music

"The reason we couldn't get anything was that I was scared, and when you're scared you can't breathe right. And besides the songs weren't my kind of thing."

—*Referring to his first formal recording session at Sun Records*

"I sang then with a big heavy rhythm—what I called a rockabilly beat."

—*Describing his early style of singing*

Driving his sports car around Las Vegas in April 1956

"I don't know what all the fuss is about. I'm just a guy who makes music—no different from anybody else."

Sam Phillips: "You hold on to what you did there."
Elvis: "What did I do? What did I do?"
Sam Phillips: "It was all so instinctive that he simply didn't know."

—*Elvis after an early Sun recording session*

"When my first record came out I was leery of it. I thought everybody would laugh."

"I thought people would laugh at me. Some did, and some are still laughing today, I guess."

> —*Explaining why he went to the movies instead of listening to his song being played on the radio for the first time*

"I've always been a dreamer. When I was young I used to read comic books and go to the movies and I was the hero. My dreams have come true a hundred times over."

"The people were looking for something different and I came along just in time. I was lucky."

"Sure, Colonel, whatever you say is okay with me."

—*To his manager, Colonel Tom Parker*

"We're the perfect combination. Colonel's an old carny, and me, I'm off the wall."

1034 Audubon Drive, Memphis (1956)

Wearing his favorite plaid sport coat (1956)

"He's the only guy that really gave me the big breaks. . . . I don't think I would have ever been very big with another man. Because he's—he's a very smart man."

—Talking about Colonel Parker in 1955

"Colonel Parker is more or less like a daddy when I'm away from my own folks. He doesn't meddle in my affairs. Ain't nobody can tell me 'you do this or that.' Colonel Parker knows the business and I don't. He never butts into record sessions, I don't butt into business. Nobody can tell you how to run your life."

"I don't compare my girlfriends with my mother."

☆ ☆ ☆

"Guess I like dating more than anything."

—*Talking about his favorite pastime*

"I haven't given marriage much thought. I like to date girls who are fun to be with."

☆ ☆ ☆

Question: "What kind of girls do you prefer?"
Elvis: "Female mostly."

"Women should be treated like ladies."

☆ ☆ ☆

"I look forward to our marriage and a little Elvis. I have never and never again will love anyone like I love you."

—*To Anita Wood*

"Which one is more nervous, you or me?"

> —*To June Juanico while they were necking on the*
> *White House Hotel pier*

☆ ☆ ☆

"If I had to drop it all, I could do it, but I wouldn't like it."

Shooting clay pigeons at Ocean Springs, Mississippi. Longtime friend Red West is at Elvis's elbow.

"Johnny, someday I'm going to be driving Cadillacs."

     —To his friend Johnny Slack in 1952

"Man, if I could ever get people to talk about me the way they talk about Liberace, I would really have it made."

     —At the Eagle's Nest Nightclub

"That boy can go! I think he has a great future ahead of him . . . and the way he plays piano just gets inside of me."

—*Talking about Jerry Lee Lewis*

"You know those people in New York are not gonna change me none. I'm gonna show you what the real Elvis is like tonight."

—*To a crowd at Russwood Park, Memphis, in July 1956*

"I got wired the wrong way."

—*Talking about once becoming an electrician*

"Mama, I don't want to go. These people got a lot of money and I don't fit in. I don't feel comfortable. I just don't want to go."

—*Responding to an invitation to a wealthy Memphis family for dinner*

"When I was a boy, I was the hero in comic books and movies. I grew up believing in a dream. Now, I've lived it out. That's all a man can ask for."

"Not me, I'm not taking any chances. They just might train that thing—whatever it is—right out of my throat."

　　—*Why Elvis didn't want to take voice lessons*

Peabody Hotel, Memphis, in July 1956

"When I was a kid I'd sit on our porch and watch those long, low cars whiz by. I told myself then that when I was grown, I was gonna have me, not one, but two Cadillacs sitting out front of Mama's and Daddy's house. Well sir, I guess you can say I've done a little better than that."

"I just don't know what it is. Only the other day, Daddy looked at me and said, 'What happened, El? The last thing I remember is that I was working in a little ol' paint factory and you were driving a truck.'"

"That was the best five
bucks I ever spent."

—*Thinking back to his first record*

Elvis donated FDR's yacht, Potomac, *to comedian Danny Thomas. The vessel was auctioned off to benefit Thomas's favorite charity, St. Jude's Children's Hospital.*

MEET THE PRESS

At THE BEGINNING OF his career, Elvis Presley faced an onslaught of media attention. Because his style of music and presentation was so new, so foreign, he was constantly defending himself against being labeled "vulgar" or a "juvenile delinquent."

Elvis literally had to convince church and civic groups across the country that he was an ordinary, decent, churchgoing country boy who just happened to love to sing rock 'n' roll music.

As his popularity soared, the media adjusted to Elvis's style and began to accept him. And to his fans, Elvis was a voice that spoke for their generation.

It became evident with hit after hit that Elvis Presley wasn't just another fad.

"Well, everything has happened to me so fast during the past year and a half. I'm all mixed up, you know. I can't keep up with everything that's happened."

—*To Hy Gardner in July 1856 about his sudden rise to popularity*

"I thought it was supposed to get easier, but it's getting worse. I hate having to read what people write 'bout me. I just hate it."

"Well, sir, you got to accept the bad along with the good. . . . I know that I'm doing the best I can."

—*To Hy Gardner during an interview*

"They don't bother me none. And I'm figuring to stay around for a long time."

—*Talking about critics*

"I happened to come along at a time in the music business when there was no trend. I was lucky. The people were looking for something different. I came along just in time."

—*Talking to the press*

"I don't feel I'm doing anything wrong."

Wearing his famous gold lamé jacket on tour in Canada (1957)

57

After being discharged from the army, Elvis gave his first interview while on a train to Memphis.

Question: "Are you thinking about doing something different, like running for public office?"

Elvis: "No sir. I don't have aspirations in politics or anything of that nature."

"I ain't no saint but I've tried never to do anything that would hurt my family or offend God. . . . I figure all any kid needs is hope and the feeling he or she belongs. If I could do or say anything that would give some kid that feeling, I would believe I had contributed something to the world."

—*To a Memphis reporter in the 1950s*

"I don't do no dirty body movements."

  —*Responding to charges that he was impairing the morals of minors*

☆ ☆ ☆

"I can't figure out what I'm doing wrong. I know my mother approves of what I do."

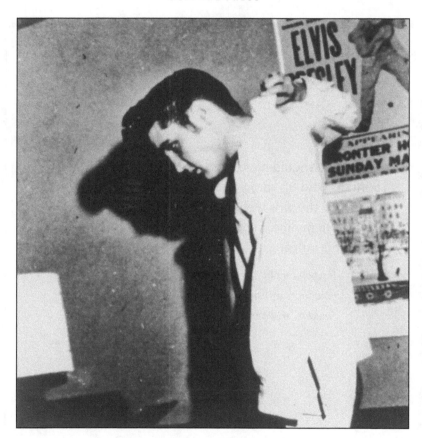

New Frontier Hotel, Las Vegas (April 1956)

"Baby, you should have been there. Every time D. J. [Fontana] did his thing on the drums, I wiggled my finger and the girls went wild. I never heard screams like that in my life. I showed them sons of bitches calling me vulgar."

—*Responding to juvenile court judge Marion Gooding's instructions that Elvis restrain his "vulgar" movements*

"I wouldn't do anything vulgar in front of anybody . . . . My folks didn't bring me up that way. I just move with the music. It's the way I feel."

"Some make me feel so bad I can't hardly sleep at night. I shouldn't let it worry me, but I can't help it. What gets me really sore is the way they try to smear the kids as delinquents who go for my stuff. What's the matter with grownups today? What are they scared of? Why do they get so upset whenever teenagers get a chance to express how they feel?"

—*Responding to critics*

Talking to reporters after his controversial performance at Fort Homer Westerly Armory in Tampa, Florida (August 5, 1956)

"There was some article that came out where I got the jumping around from my religion. Well, my religion has nothing to do with what I do now. Because the type of stuff I do now is not religious music, and my religious background has nothing to do with the way I sing."

☆ ☆ ☆

"They'll all get theirs!"

—*Talking about television ministers*

"I don't do any vulgar movements. I'm not trying to be sexy. It's just my way of expressing how I feel when I move around. My movements are all leg movements with my body."

"Sir, those kids that come here and pay their money to see this show come to have a good time."

—*To* Tampa Tribune *reporter Paul Wilder*

"No sir, I don't like them to call me 'Elvis the Pelvis.' It's the most childish expression I've ever heard from an adult, 'Elvis the Pelvis,' but if they want to call me that, there's nothing I can do about it. You just have to accept the good with the bad."

"When I sang hymns back home with Mom and Pop I stood still and I looked like you feel when you sang a hymn. When I sing this rock 'n' roll, my eyes won't stay open and my legs won't stand still. I don't care what they say, it ain't nasty."

"I can't help it. I just have to jump around when I sing. But it ain't vulgar. It's just the way I feel. I don't feel sexy when I'm singing—if that were true, I'd be in some kind of institution as some kind of sex maniac."

"Sometimes every knock can be a boost. When everybody agrees on something and someone says, 'I like that,' they start talking about something else. When there's no controversy, there's no news. When they quit talking about you, you're dead."

"A lot of these guys aren't reporters, they're marksmen."

☆ ☆ ☆

"I want to do everything to keep people liking me. I don't want any more bad write-ups."

"I could make you like me if I tried. I'm just teasing now, but I'd be sweet, and you'd like me because I was sweet, wouldn't you?"

—*Flirting with women reporters*

Elvis: "Mama, do you really think I'm vulgar on stage?"

Gladys: "Son you're not vulgar, but seems to me you're putting too much into your singing. Keep that up and you won't live to be thirty."

Louisiana Hayride *performance* (1955)

71

"There are low-down people and high-up people, but all of them get the kind of feeling this rock 'n' roll music tells about."

—*Responding to criticism of his style*

Hy : "Do you feel any animosity toward your critics?"

Elvis: "Well, not really. Those people have a job to do, and they do it."

Hy: "Have you learned anything from them?"

Elvis: "No, I haven't."

Hy: "You haven't, huh?"

Elvis: "I don't feel like I'm doing anything wrong."

—*From a 1956 interview with Hy Gardner*

"It's all great. I've been looking forward to this homecoming very much. I've been escorted out of these fairgrounds when I was a kid and snuck in over the fence. But this is the first time I've been escorted in."

—*At a press conference at the Tupelo Mississippi/ Alabama State Fair on September 26, 1956*

"I admire the man. He has a right to say what he wants to say. He is a great success and a fine actor, but I think he shouldn't have said it. He's mistaken about this. This is a trend, just the same as he faced when he started years ago. I consider it the greatest music."

—*Commenting on Frank Sinatra's extreme comments on rock 'n' roll*

Rare backstage shot in the gold lamé suit (1956)

"Lots of people make fun of what they call 'Holy Rollers.' They look on them as ignorant and not really religious at all. In the church we belong to, we really feel our religion and get carried away with it. We're not ashamed to show it. I think spirituals are the best songs in the world; they got a beat and folks down our way really feel that music. Someday I'm gonna record me some spirituals."

Question: "How do you manage to keep so young?"

Elvis: "I really don't know. One of these days it will catch up with me and I'll probably fall apart."

Question: "Why do you think you've outlasted every
other performer from the '50s?"

Elvis: "I take vitamin E."

☆ ☆ ☆

Question: "Are you tired of the old stuff [music]?"

Elvis: "I'm not the least bit ashamed of 'Hound
Dog' or 'Heartbreak Hotel.'"

IN THE ARMY NOW

During the production of *King Creole*, Elvis Presley received his draft notice. He was allowed to finish the picture before his induction and deployment overseas to Germany.

Elvis had mixed feelings about being in the army. On the one hand, he felt proud to represent his country, but on the other, he felt the timing of being drafted couldn't have come at a worse time.

His career was going full steam, and he felt that his absence would only hurt his popularity. Other fears for him were being away from his family and friends and facing a totally new lifestyle. Also during that time, his mother died.

After his return from Germany, Elvis headed for Hollywood to resume his film career. His fears about his career dying were short-lived when fans welcomed him home with open arms.

"There should be no draft."

—*To the Memphis press*

"Had to. Got a job at Loew's State Theater in Memphis as an usher. They fired me for fighting in the lobby. I've worked in factories, drove a truck, cut grass for a living, and did a hitch in a defense plant. I'll do whatever they [the army] tell me, and I won't be asking for no special favors."

—*Talking to columnist Vernon Scott in 1957*

"Every able-bodied American boy should go into the service. And I am an able-bodied American boy, so why not?"

☆ ☆ ☆

"I'm going to be a good soldier or bust."

Army interview, Germany (October 1, 1958)

"I'll go [into the army] when they call me."

☆ ☆ ☆

"[G]ratitude] . . . for what this country has given me.
And now I'm ready to return a little. It's the only adult
way to look at it."

—*Upon receiving his draft notice*

"When I get back to being a civilian again, I hope I'll be able to take up my career where I left off. That is, if my fans want it that way."

Jimmy Page: "Would you like to go into Special
　　　　　　　 Services?"

Elvis: "I want to go where I can do the best job. I'll
　　　　 do what I have to—like any American boy."

—*In a* Memphis Press-Scimitar *interview*

"I want to go where I can do the best job for the army.
I'll go where they want me, when they want me."

☆ ☆ ☆

"I don't know if I'll be doing any singing in the army,
haven't so far. . . . I guess the army knows best."

"It's human nature to gripe, but I'm going ahead and doing the best I can. One thing the army teaches is boys to think like men."

☆ ☆ ☆

"Isn't it only right that the draft should apply to everybody alike? Rich or poor, there should be no exceptions."

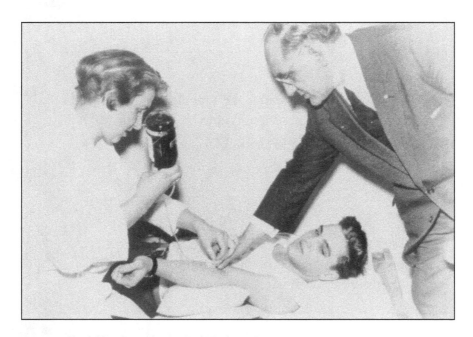

Donating blood, like other soldiers, at Bad Nauheim, Germany (1958)

"All I want is to be treated like a regular GI. I want to do my duty, and I'm mighty proud to be given the opportunity to serve my country."

—*To his army buddies*

"Well, any mother hates to see her son go into the service. My mother is no different from millions of other mothers who hated to see their sons go."

"Hair today, gone tomorrow."

*—Comment as fifty-five reporters and photographers
watched his hair being cut for army induction*

☆ ☆ ☆

"My hair is my trademark. I never meant to offend
anyone with it. But people have been making such a big
to-do with my keeping my hair. I don't want any
partiality. I don't want to go into the service and have
the rest of the boys in short hair and me in long hair.
All GI's get crewcuts."

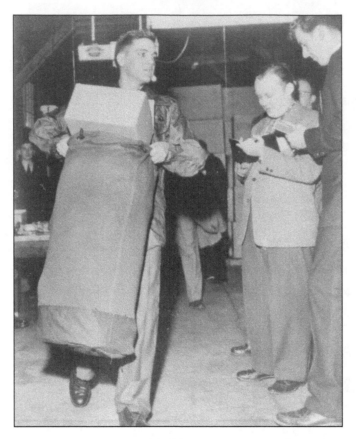

Picking up his gear at Fort Chaffee, Arkansas, on March 25, 1958

"I'm looking forward to [going to] Germany. I'm looking forward to seeing the country and meeting a lot of the people, but at the same time I'm looking forward to coming back here, because here is where I started."

"Yep, I'm getting married. To the U.S. Army."

"I'm going into that service and do the best I can. If they want me to sing for the boys, I'll sing. If they want me to march—anything they want me to do is all right."

"I look upon my reporting to the army this way. It'll be a relief. It won't be a snap, I know, but it'll give me a chance to unwind, to catch my breath."

"It's all over [his career]. They aren't going to know me when I get back."

☆ ☆ ☆

"It's more or less a challenge and it's a different life. The only way to cut it is to play it straight. I just stick to my job. I don't do any entertaining or make any appearances or even cut any records."

Friedberg, Germany (March 2, 1960)

"Oh, no sir, not at all. I kinda expected it because even out in civilian life I get harassed a little bit by a few people, you know, and I expected it in there. But when those guys looked around, they saw me pulling KP and marching with a pack on my back and everything. Then they figured, 'Well he's just like we are.' So I got along very well with them. And they're a good bunch of guys."

"Everybody keeps asking what I'll do in the army, and I tell them I'll do whatever I'm asked. I drove a truck once, and I can do it again if they want me to. But whatever it is, I won't ask for special favors. I plan to do my job the best I know how."

"I put in for combat maneuvers because I didn't want any mother writing in to ask, 'Why do you get out of things my boy has to do.'"

☆ ☆ ☆

"I miss my buddies back home. You can't go through life depending on other people. In the army you learn to depend on yourself."

Even the king of rock 'n' roll had to carry his own duffel at Bremerhaven on October 1, 1958.

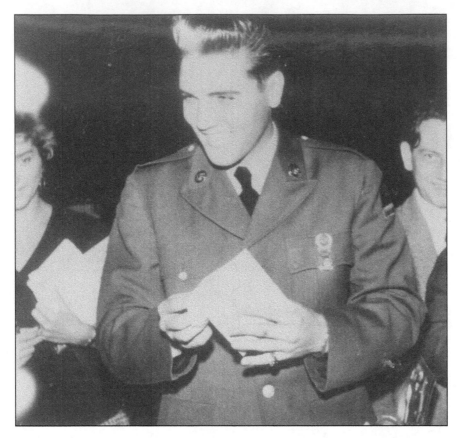

Germany (1958)

Question: "Are you going to make the army your career?"

Elvis: "Well it's gonna be my career as long as I'm in it."

☆ ☆ ☆

Question: "Do you have any regrets about leaving the army?"

Elvis: "Yes. You make friends in the army that you'll remember the rest of your life."

—*In a post-army interview*

"I still think of her every single, solitary day. If I never do anything that's really wrong or bad, it'll be because of Mama. She wouldn't never let me do anything wrong."

"If I could have one wish granted it would be to talk again with my mother. There are times I dream about her. She's always happy and smiling. Sometimes we embrace, and it's so real I wake up in a cold sweat."

At a piano in Germany (left) and outside his rental home at Bad Nauheim in 1958 (right)

"It wasn't only like losing a mother, it was like losing a friend, a companion, someone I could talk to."

"I've lived my whole life just for you. Oh, God! Everything I have is gone."

—*Standing at his mother's coffin*

"The bottom dropped out
of my life the day my
mother died. I thought that
I had nothing left. In a way
I was right."

"It was good, but I was so hungry I'd eat anything this morning."

—*Regarding his first breakfast in the army*

"I've eaten things in the army that I never ate before. And I've eaten things that I didn't know what it was, but after a hard day of basic training, you could eat a rattlesnake."

"I love the fans. I love the pretty girls. When they come running to me, I want to run to them, not away from them. I hope they don't blame me when army regulations force me to look straight ahead on duty. I want them to know I'm not ignoring them."

"I like the continental look, with slash pockets and thin-legged pants."

—*Commenting about fashion in a post-army interview*

"I've learned a lot about people in the army. There was all different types. I never lived with other people before and had a chance to find out how they think. It sure changed me, but I can't tell offhand just how."

"If I say the army made a man of me, it would give the impression I was an idiot before I was drafted. I wasn't exactly that."

Army interview, Bremerhaven, Germany (1958)

107

"Everything was just straight down the middle. I was treated no better or no worse than any of the other boys. And that's the way I wanted it because I have to live with the other boys, you know."

☆ ☆ ☆

Question: "Do you plan to reenlist?"

Elvis: "Good Lord, no. My manager would probably cut my throat."

"I've learned one thing in this man's army. Man, coming home is the greatest!"

☆ ☆ ☆

"I'll fall in love someday and maybe there'll be a rock 'n' roll wedding."

—*On his return from the army*

"Guys, I've just met the
prettiest girl I've ever seen.
Her name is Priscilla.
Someday I'll probably
marry her."

Question: "Did you find European girls any different
from American girls?"

Elvis: "Girls are girls as far as I'm concerned."

—In a post-army interview

Question: "Why have you changed your hairstyle?"

Elvis: "It's like a car you've driven in for a couple
of years—it's just time for a change."

—In a post-army interview

Smooching Dolores Hart, Elvis's costar in the film Loving You

HOORAY FOR HOLLYWOOD

MORE THAN ANYTHING, Elvis Presley wanted "to be a good actor," as he once said.

During the ten years that Elvis lived in Hollywood he made thirty-three films. All of them featured what Hollywood felt was his greatest talent: singing.

Elvis showed real promise to be a good actor but was never given an opportunity to showcase his talents.

As he completed picture after picture, he soon became disillusioned with Hollywood. He felt his movies were silly and trivial. Elvis wanted more dramatic roles. But box-office appeal kept him in movies that costarred popular leading ladies and featured lukewarm plots and plenty of songs. But always the professional, Elvis gave 110 percent to each film he starred in.

"I'd like to become a good actor. That's my ambition."

☆ ☆ ☆

"I'd like to have the ability of James Dean . . . but I'd never compare myself to James Dean."

☆ ☆ ☆

"If I had to find one place to live—just one—and it couldn't be Graceland, then it would be Hollywood."

Posing with two film executives on the set of the Twentieth Century Fox film Flaming Star *(released December 20, 1960)*

115

Posing with actress Irish McCalla, star of the '50s television show Sheena, Queen of the Jungle. *Both were guests on* The Milton Berle Show.

116

"Am I a rock 'n' roller and a balladeer or a movie actor? I feel I can do both and not let one interfere with the other. I stop thinking of my guitar when I step on a movie stage."

—*On his career in 1956*

"I'll never make it, it will never happen because they're never going to hear me 'cause they're screaming all the time."

—*After reading the review for* Love Me Tender

117

"It's something I didn't ever think would happen to me, of all people. It just shows you can never tell what's going to happen to you in life."

—*On getting a movie contract*

☆ ☆ ☆

"How can you help but put your heart and soul into this?"

—*Commenting on love scenes*

"I've got an awfully long way to go yet. I don't have any method. I've never been to dramatic classes or any coach, and I still have my Southern accent."

On location for King Creole, *with costar Carolyn Jones, filmed right before Elvis went into the army (Lake Pontchartrain, Louisiana, 1957)*

119

Publicity shot on location for the 1968 MGM film Stay Away Joe. *Most of the movie was filmed in Sedona, Arizona.*

"I want to become a good actor because you can't build a whole career on just singing. Look at Frank Sinatra, until he added acting to singing, he found himself slipping downhill."

☆ ☆ ☆

"I'm pretty bad. That's something you learn through practice."

☆ ☆ ☆

"I don't ever want to stop singing, but more than anything I want to be an actor."

☆ ☆ ☆

"I never met Jimmy Dean, but how I wish I had."

"Oh, my God. I shook hands with Marlon Brando!"

> —*After bumping into Brando at the*
> *Paramount commissary*

☆ ☆ ☆

"After my first picture for Hal Wallis, it's non-musicals for me!"

☆ ☆ ☆

"I've had people ask me what I'm going to sing in the movie, and I'm not. I mean, not as far as I know."

> —*Talking about his role in* Love Me Tender

Sexy scene with starlet Jana Lund in the film Loving You *(1957)*

Looking at publicity photos on location for his first film, Love Me Tender *(1956)*

"It was quite a challenge for me because it was written for a more experienced actor."

   —Commenting on his role in King Creole

☆ ☆ ☆

"I want to go to Hollywood and become the next James Dean."

☆ ☆ ☆

"I always criticize myself in films. I'm always striving to be natural in front of a camera. That takes studying, of a sort."

"I knew my script. They sent it to me before I came to Hollywood . . . and I got out there and just tried to put myself in the place of the character I was playing, just trying to act as naturally as I could."

—*Commenting on his screen test for* Rainmaker

"Well, I would like to play a dramatic role, but I don't—I'm not ready for that either, really. I haven't had enough experience in acting; and until I'm ready for it, it would be foolish to undertake something very dramatic."

Talking to costar Dolores Hart on the set of Loving You

Elvis made the switch to comedy in the 1962 United Artists film Follow That Dream. *He played Toby Kwimper, a Lil' Abner type, with costars Anne Helm and Arthur O'Connell.*

"All my life, I've wanted to be an actor. Though I was never in any school plays. Always sticking in the back of my head was the idea that somehow, someday, I'd get a chance to act."

☆ ☆ ☆

"I'm trying to make it in acting, you know. And it takes a long time, a lot of work, and a lot of experience. But I'm trying to make it that way, and if I can get established that way, I'm okay. But I don't know how long the music end of it will last. I don't know how long I'll last. I've got no idea really."

"If I were a good actor, I think I would like it [being in films] a little better. Although if I ever break into acting completely, I'll still continue singing. I'll still continue to make records."

☆ ☆ ☆

Jackie Gleason: "You keep calling me 'Sir' or 'Mister Gleason.' Why don't you call me 'Jackie' like everybody else?"

Elvis: "Well, when I was a little boy, Mama told me that anybody one year older than I was 'Mister,' and Mr. Gleason, you're one year older than I am, sir—I think."

Joking with Jackie Gleason on the set of Girls, Girls, Girls. *Costar Laurel Goodwin stands behind Elvis (1962).*

131

On location for one of his biggest movie hits, Blue Hawaii. *Here Elvis plays with a Welsh Corgi between scenes.*

"I have no trouble memorizing. I once memorized General MacArthur's farewell speech, and I can still reel off Lincoln's Gettysburg speech from when I memorized it in school."

☆ ☆ ☆

"I'm not after big excitement on a weekend after working hard all week. I'm not much for night-clubbing."

☆ ☆ ☆

"I don't really like parties . . . I don't like loud noise, and I don't smoke or drink."

—*Why Elvis didn't go to Hollywood parties (1959)*

"How can you enjoy it when you have to sing songs to the guy you've just punched out."

Question: "What kind of a part do you play in *Speedway?*"

Elvis: "I'm kind of a singing millionaire-playboy race driver, sir."

Question: "Have you assayed such a part before?"

Elvis: "Only about twenty-five times, sir."

"I look at my old movies and I can pick up on my mistakes. There's a lot I'd like to change."

Doing what made his movies reliable moneymakers—belting out songs and looking handsome

In Blue Hawaii, *costar Jennie Maxwell played a spoiled teen with a crush on Elvis. The movie was filmed at several locations in Hawaii, including Waikiki Beach.*

136

"I wasn't exactly James Bond in that movie, but then no one ever asked Sean Connery to sing while dodging bullets."

☆ ☆ ☆

"What can you do with a piece of #~&% like this?"

—*Commenting on the* Double Trouble *soundtrack*

☆ ☆ ☆

"Maybe one day we'll do one right."

—*After the making of* Harum Scarum

☆ ☆ ☆

"The only thing that's worse than watching a bad movie is being in one."

137

"If you have ten songs in a picture, they can't be all good. Like, when you have to sing to a turtle—what kind of song is that?"

"I've made a study of poor Jimmy Dean. I've made a study of myself. And I know why girls, at least the young ones, go for us. We're sullen, we're brooding, we're something of a menace. I don't understand it exactly, but that's what the girls like in men. I don't know anything about Hollywood, but I know you can't be sexy if you smile. You can't be real if you grin."

"I'm not going to quit, and I'm not going to take [acting] lessons because I want to be me."

In Girls, Girls, Girls (1962), *Elvis played a carefree bachelor who worked on a charter boat.*

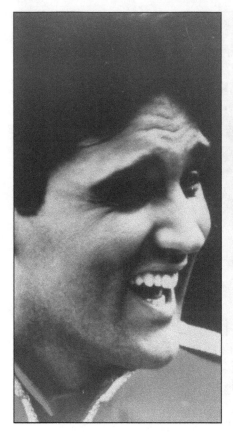 

Scenes from the 1966 film Frankie and Johnny. *The film was loosely based on the song.*

"Hollywood, a lovely city . . . but home for me will always spell Memphis and Graceland."

☆ ☆ ☆

"The girl I marry will have to consider her home Memphis, not Hollywood."

☆ ☆ ☆

Question: "What kind of girls do you like?"
    Elvis: "A lot of different types—actresses and
        schoolgirls."

☆ ☆ ☆

"I can't go on doing the same thing year after year. The inspiration simply isn't there."

"One thing I gotta do is go after more serious material. Anyway, I'm real tired of playing a fella who gets into a fight, then starts singing to the guy he's just beat up."

"I wasn't ready for that town and it wasn't ready for me."

"I got hung up in Hollywood making pictures and got away from the people."

Question: "Why do you dye your hair?"
    Elvis: "I just done it for the movie 'cause it's really gray."

Posing with a celebration cake at the cast party for Wild in the Country (1961)

143

Signing autographs at the Weeki Wachee Springs Water Park (July 30, 1961)

FAME, FORTUNE & FANS

AT A VERY EARLY age, Elvis Presley felt the aches and pains of poverty. As one of the top performers of the twentieth century, he soon had more money then he ever thought possible.

Elvis was a generous man who shared his wealth with others less fortunate: family, friends, and even strangers. To Elvis it simply didn't matter how he spent his money as long as it made others happy.

Elvis also loved the admiration of his fans. He loved to entertain them. But with all the fame and fortune he achieved, Elvis was a lonely man. The pressures he faced as Elvis the "entertainer" soon took its toll on Elvis the "human being."

Whatever his situation, Elvis's loyalty to his fans was evident. They were his top priority because he felt a bond with them and believed they were largely responsible for his success.

"You say no to one person because you had a hundred autographs to sign, they just know you're saying no to them. I never refuse to do anything like that, no matter how tired I am."

"The Lord can give . . . the Lord can take away. I might be herding sheep next year."

"I don't know how long it will last. When it's gone I'll switch to something else. I would like to sing ballads the way Eddie Fisher does and the way Perry Como does. But the way I'm singing now is what makes the money. Would you change if you were me?"

"Well, I don't mind. Without them I'd be . . . lost."

—*Referring to fans following him*

"I wish I could just do that [walk away from the life he was leading]. It's too late for that. There are too many people. There are too many people who depend on me. I'm too obligated. I'm in too far to get out!"

"It's all happening so fast, there's so much happening to me . . . that some nights I just can't fall asleep. It scares me, you know . . . it just scares me."

"I'll bet I could burp and make them squeal."

☆ ☆ ☆

"I wonder how many of my friends that are here now would be here if it were five years ago. Not very many, because they are all looking for something from me."

☆ ☆ ☆

"Pastor, I am the most miserable young man you have ever seen. I have got more money than I can ever spend. I have thousands of fans out there, and I have a lot of people who call themselves my friends, but I am miserable. I am not doing a lot of things you taught me, and I'm doing some things you taught me not to do."

—*Talking to the Reverend James Hamill, First Assembly of God Church, Memphis*

Signing autographs in Tampa, Florida (August 5, 1956)

The Cool King lunches on ice cream while mingling with fans in Tampa, Florida.

"I have not sold my soul to the devil. It's only music!"

☆ ☆ ☆

Question: "Have you made any contributions to culture?"

Elvis: "Like income taxes, you mean?"

☆ ☆ ☆

"Everything is going so fine for me that I can't believe it's not a dream. I hope I never wake up."

☆ ☆ ☆

"We pay the price for fame with our nerves, don't we?"

—*To John Lennon*

Elvis: "It's lonesome, T."

Tommy: "How can you talk about that with thousands of people . . ."

Elvis: "Well, I can't go get a hamburger. I can't go in some greasy joint. I can't go water skiing or shopping."

—*Talking to Tommy Cutrer, promoter for the Grand Ole Opry, in 1957*

"Advice to teenagers? All I can say is if I do anything wrong, don't copy me."

Posing with excited fans on one of his early tours in the South. His tour bus is in background.

Joking with friends and fans in Tampa, Florida (1956)

Press: "How do you combine marriage and
show business?"

Elvis: "Very carefully, very carefully."

☆ ☆ ☆

"When you're behind the wheel, you're in charge of
everything that's going on. You're free to just go."

☆ ☆ ☆

"Oh yeah, my gold record."

—*Response after receiving yet another gold record*

"I just take every day as it comes. I don't plan too far ahead. There'll be record albums, of course, and movies too. Don't know anymore, maybe I'll go back to driving a truck."

"Ya gotta sell what ya feel. That's success, man!"

"When you're the top gunslinger in town, everyone takes you on."

"It's not how much you have that makes people look up to you, it's who you are."

Signing an autograph on the hood of his Caddy in Tampa, Florida (1956)

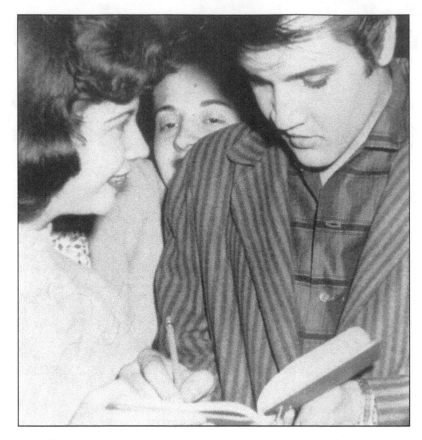

Elvis probably signed more autographs than any celebrity then or now (1956)

"My audience is changing. . . . They don't move as fast as they used to."

—Commenting on the fact that most of his early fans were now married with families of their own

☆ ☆ ☆

"Love and marriage are the most important things in life. Even more important than one's career."

☆ ☆ ☆

"Mama would see the girls mobbing me, and she'd get upset—but I told her they just like me."

"Teenagers are my life and triumph. I'd be nowhere without them."

☆ ☆ ☆

"I've learned a lot about loneliness."

☆ ☆ ☆

"It's lonely at the top, but, God, I love that lonely feeling."

☆ ☆ ☆

"I only really feel at home in Memphis, at my own Graceland Mansion. . . . A man gets lonesome for the things that are familiar to him—my friends and acquaintances."

Posing with fans while on location for **King Creole** *(Lake Pontchartrain, Louisiana)*

Signing an autograph for a Belgian fan (Las Vegas, 1973)

"You know, when some people get down and out, they go out and get drunk and forget it all. Me, I just go out and buy another car. I've got money and I could buy anything there is to buy, but I still can't get out and mix with people like I'd like to."

☆ ☆ ☆

Question: "A penny for your thoughts?"
Elvis: "Money can't buy what I want."

☆ ☆ ☆

"Retirement? Well, I'll put it like this. I'll never quit as long as I'm doing okay. As long as you're pleasing the public, you'd be foolish to quit."

"You gotta prove yourself,
prove yourself,
prove yourself!"

☆ ☆ ☆

"It isn't so difficult to discover who your real friends are if they're around long enough. If I find out someone sticks with me just to see what he can get out of it, I ease him out of the circle."

FAME, FORTUNE & FANS

Tampa, Florida (1956)

165

"I've always liked challenges. I like to prove I'm better than I was yesterday. There's no fun in making a hit unless you deserve it. I believe in that, and I'm trying to live by it."

"I'm not shooting for a certain number of millions of dollars. If you do that, then you put money ahead of doing your job."

"They aren't employees. These boys are my friends from down home. I've known them since we were kids."

—*On the "Memphis Mafia"*

"I do try hard to please my fans, not just for the money it brings me, but because I like show business. There's a great personal satisfaction in performing when fans appreciate you."

☆ ☆ ☆

"Money's meant to be spread around. The more happiness it helps create, the more it's worth. It's worthless as old paper if it just lies in a bank and grows there without having been used to help anybody."

☆ ☆ ☆

"I don't mind if the fans rip the shirt from my back— they put it there."

"Those fellows went to school with me. There were my friends. And now they don't even stop to talk."

—When Elvis was snubbed by an old Memphis friend

"You can't fool yourself or the public for very long."

"My success? Well, I don't know. You might say it is hard work and good luck. Something like that. Whatever it is, I hope it doesn't quit."

From babies to grandmas, Elvis gave out kisses along with autographs. (Weeki Wachee, Florida, July 1961)

"Sometimes my teeth get tired of smiling. It's doggone tiring. But it's worth it. After all, you can't knock success."

"I've made some wonderful friends in the so-called grandmother group. They write the greatest letters. I even try to see them when possible. They're real fun people."

"People keep saying that my manager has a good thing in me, taking 25 percent of my earnings. He sure has. And I've got myself a good thing in him. We both make money. He knows how to drive a hard bargain for me. And he works night and day."

"I don't regard money or position as important. But I can never forget the longing to be someone. I guess if you're poor, you always think bigger and want more than fellows who have most everything from the minute they're born."

"I've been scratched and bitten and everything. I just accept it with a broad smile. They don't intend to hurt you. They just want a piece of you for a souvenir."

Elvis: "Colonel, you put a lump in my throat."
    Colonel Parker: "Elvis, you put a lump in my
        wallet."

☆ ☆ ☆

Question: "What do you think you'd do if rock 'n' roll
        ever died out?"
    Elvis: "Why, I'd probably just starve to death."

☆ ☆ ☆

"It's a fast life—I just can't slow down. Seems like I'm
hurrying all the time."

Hy Gardner: "How do your parents feel about your success?"

Elvis: "Well, I guess they're just like myself. They're very thankful for it. We've always had a common life. We never had any luxuries, but we were never really hungry, you know, and I guess they're just, you know, they're real proud, just like I am."

A major move in Elvis's career was a stint on The Louisiana Hayride Variety Show *(1956)*

MUSIC & CONCERTS

From his early days at *The Louisiana Hayride* to later in his career at big arenas across the country or even in Las Vegas, Elvis Presley loved to sing and perform on stage in front of a crowd of adoring fans.

He felt at home in front of a crowd. He would often laugh with them, telling when he was nervous or joking with them when he would forget the words of a song.

His musical style ranged from country and rhythm and blues to gospel and rock 'n' roll. His voice, he claimed, was a gift from God.

With sell-out concerts everywhere he performed, Elvis always put on shows that were memorable.

"I know that I get carried away with the music and the beat sometimes. And I don't quite know what I'm doing. But it's all rhythm and the beat—it's full of life. I enjoy it. The kids understand it. It's the newness. I think older people will grow to understand. It's being young—you know—this generation."

"I don't see how any type of music would have any bad influence on people. When it's only music . . . I mean how would rock 'n' roll music make people rebel against their parents?"

Elvis's wild gyrations created a storm of controversy in his early days. His fans loved every move.

The famous gold lamé suit was hot and heavy. Elvis only wore it for a short time.

178

Steve Sholes: "Okay, Elvis, I think we've got it."

Elvis: "I hope so, Mr. Sholes."

Steve Sholes: "Elvis, you ready to hear the playback?"

Elvis: "Now's as good a time as any."

—During the thirty-first take of "Hound Dog," Elvis could be heard saying, "This is the one."

"Boy this is my favorite music. When I'm out there [on stage] I do what they want to hear. When I'm back here, I can do what I want to do."

—Referring to gospel music in 1954

179

"The guitar sounded like somebody beating on a bucket lid."

—*Commenting on his first recording, "My Happiness"*

"[This music was] the real thing right from the heart."

"Mr. Phillips [of Sun Records] I just feel like . . . I failed."

—*After a performance at the Bon Air Club, July 17, 1954*

The gold lamé suit is now displayed in the Graceland Museum.

181

Looking to the heavens for divine guidance or at screaming fans in the balcony?

"The only time I feel alive . . . is when I'm in front of my audience, my people. That's the only time I really feel like a human being."

☆ ☆ ☆

"I don't know, it's hard to explain. It's like your whole body gets goose bumps, but it's not goose bumps. It's not a chill either. It's like a surge of electricity going through you. It's almost like making love, but it's even stronger than that."

—*Commenting on his stage style*

"Rock 'n' roll music, if you like it, if you feel it, you can't help but move to it. That's what's happening to me. I can't help it. I have to move around. I can't stand still. I've tried it and I can't do it."

☆ ☆ ☆

"Colonel Parker said 'If I Can Dream' wasn't an Elvis kind of song. I'd like to try it, man."

☆ ☆ ☆

"It's all a big hoax. . . . I get one-third of the credit for recording it. It makes me look smarter than I am."

Elvis was a complete natural for the camera (Canada, 1957)

Performing "If I Can Dream" on the 1968 television special

"Thanks, man, for the early lessons you gave me."

—*Talking to blues legend B. B. King*

☆ ☆ ☆

"I lose myself in my singing. Maybe it's my early training singing gospel hymns. I'm limp as a rag, worn out, when the show's over."

—*At the Pacific Northwest Tour*

☆ ☆ ☆

"Country music was always a part of the influence on my type of music. It's a combination of country music, gospel, rhythm and blues. As a child, I was influenced by all of that."

"Mr. Parker says more people will be seeing me on these four shows [*The Dorsey Brothers Show*] than I would be exposed to for the rest of my life on the *Hayride!*"

—*Speaking to* Louisiana Hayride *performers*

Elvis: "Man, this is a good crowd in this part of the country. Are they always that way?"

Tom Perryman: "No, man. They've never seen anything like you."

—*After an early Northwest Texas show, being interviewed by DJ Tom Perryman*

Posing with blues singers Little Junior Parker (left) and Bobby "Blue" Biand (right) (1956)

Sin City wasn't prepared for Elvis and his style of music in 1956. But that didn't slow him down.

"I have a reverence for God, Mama, but it's just music. It makes me feel this way."

☆ ☆ ☆

"My first love is spiritual music—some of the old colored spirituals from way back. I know practically every religious song that's ever been written."

☆ ☆ ☆

"What I do is, I wiggle my shoulders and I shake my legs and I walk up and down the stage and hop on one foot. . . . I'd never do anything that was vulgar before an audience. My mother would never allow it."

"This is my first live appearance in nine years. I've appeared dead a few times."

—*Referring to his first stage appearance in Las Vegas in 1969*

"My style hasn't changed—only my material."

"I watch my audience and I listen to them, and I know that we're all getting something out of our systems, but none of us knows what it is."

In 1969 the King returned to Vegas.

Elvis made two documentaries on his stage career. That's the Way It Is *was a huge success.*

"Okay, I've done those movies, I've had a smash TV special. . . . I'm ready to cut some hit records."

☆ ☆ ☆

"You have to put on a show to draw a crowd."

☆ ☆ ☆

"I'm not kidding myself—my voice alone is just an ordinary voice. What people come to see is how I use it."

☆ ☆ ☆

"You know, some things just change. I just can't do it like I did."

—*Referring to his stage style changing and developing*

"People say I'm vulgar. They say I use my hips disgustingly. But that's my way of putting over a song. I have to move. When I have a lot of energy, I move more. I lose three to four pounds a performance. I've always done it that way."

"I don't see anything wrong with it. I just act the way I feel. Without my left leg, I'd be dead."

"Well, it's still going strong. Lots of people are singing it now. On the other hand, there's no law that says a singer has to stick to one kind of music all his life. I think I'll be singing rock 'n' roll for a long time, but I also hope I'll be singing other styles, too."

"I've tried to figure it out. I don't see how they think it contributes to juvenile delinquency—something that's only singing and dancing. I don't see that, because, if anything, I've tried to live a straight, clean life and not set any kind of bad example."

☆ ☆ ☆

"Rock 'n' roll music is basically gospel, rhythm and blues—or it sprang from that. And people have been adding things to it, experimenting with it."

☆ ☆ ☆

"Listening to a playback can sometimes be harder then cutting the disks."

"Maybe I should start with the national anthem." [He then sings "Hound Dog."]

"I'm really glad to be back in front of a live audience. I don't think I've ever been more excited than I am tonight."

—*Commenting on his return to Las Vegas on July 31, 1969*

"I don't think I'm changing my style. I think you have to mature a little bit."

—*Referring to his stage shows in the 1960s*

Elvis's two-week stint in 1956 at the New Frontier Hotel in Las Vegas was a surprising flop. He returned in 1969 to set all-time records.

"This is where it is: right before the audience. They make me feel good and I don't mind a little noise."

☆ ☆ ☆

"Man, they [a live audience] knocked me out. I was a little nervous for the first three songs, but then I thought, 'What the heck, get with it, man, or you just might be out of a job.'"

☆ ☆ ☆

"I want you to know that I was scared to death, sir, when I did my first number for the studio audience. Let me tell you my knees were shaking, and it wasn't just from keeping time with the music. It's been so long since I worked before a live audience. But then it all came back to me, and it was just like doing one-night stands in the old days."

"It gave me a new life. I was human again. And it gave me a chance to do what I do best—sing."

☆ ☆ ☆

"I can't figure out what I'm doing wrong. I know my mother approves of what I'm doing. If I had a teenage sister I certainly would not object to her coming to watch a show like this."

☆ ☆ ☆

"Naturally, I think rock 'n' roll is the greatest music ever because it's the only thing I can do. If I was a good popular singer, I would like popular music."

Bon voyage party thrown by reporters in Bad Nauheim, Germany. Elvis was on his way home after his stint in the army.

"I was raised around spiritual music. Before I started making records I wanted to sing in a spiritual quartet. I still go to hear spiritual singers, especially in Memphis."

☆ ☆ ☆

"I liked all types of music when I was growing up. When I was in high school, I had records by Mario Lanza and the Metropolitan Opera. I just loved music."

☆ ☆ ☆

"We did 'White Christmas,' and I don't think Bing Crosby would appreciate it. We put a little beat to it. We got the reindeers rocking."

"If you play in your hometown, you don't feel like you're on tour."

☆ ☆ ☆

Question: "What about songs that are political—poverty, homeless, land of the free . . ."

Elvis: "That's fine, if it's for the right kind of song."

—*At a Houston press conference in 1969*

☆ ☆ ☆

"The audience is the other half of me."

"I looked out and saw the crowd of people, and I got weak in the knees, you know. All of a sudden it just scared me."

Question: "Do you ever pull out any of those old records from the Sun label and listen to them?"

Elvis: "They sound funny, boy. They got a lot of echo on them, man, I'll tell you."

—*At a Houston press conference in 1969*

"I just wanted to show you all this because you paid for it."

—*Showing his expensive jewelry to the audience*

Question: "Is your stage style the same as it was or have you improved on that?"

Elvis: "Well, I just do whatever I feel on stage, you know. I always did that."

—*At a Houston press conference in 1969*

"Touring is the roughest part. You do a show, come off stage and get in the car and go to another town."

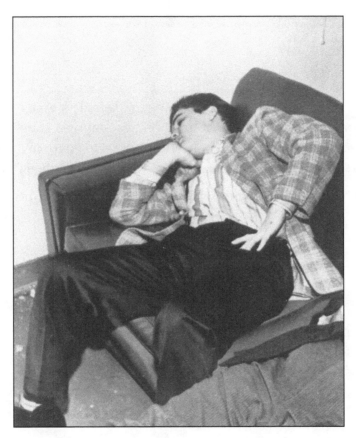

The pace of his early touring left Elvis exhausted.

"I went down there just to try out, more or less. And I went down there once. And I went back again a couple of weeks later. The people, they seemed to go for my songs a little bit. Someone gave me a job down there."

—*On getting hired to play* The Louisiana Hayride

"The RCA Victor people can tell you that when I cut my records and there's no audience to watch me, I still sing the same way—with my whole body. It's just my way of putting everything I have into a song. A doctor once told me I used up more energy in a few minutes of singing then lots of men use up in a whole working day."

"I will never abandon it [rock 'n' roll] as long as people keep appreciating it. I will never take it on my own to change. It would be a foolish mistake."

☆ ☆ ☆

"I'm doing a television special now because we figure the time is right and today's music is right. Also, I thought I ought to do this special before I get too old."

☆ ☆ ☆

"It's been too long since I've done anything but make movies and cut records. I want to make some personal appearance tours. I want to see some new places and get back where the audience is."

"I used to when I first started singing, but hardly anyone came to hear me. But when I latched onto rock 'n' roll, I had it made."

—*Why Elvis went from singing ballads to rock 'n' roll*

"I just remember one day I was singing and rocking along real good, and I heard everyone out front screaming. I wondered what they were screaming about. Then I looked down and saw my legs shaking like crazy and I figured if my legs were gonna shake, and they were gonna yell and carry on . . . why, I couldn't help either."

"I never tried to hurt teenagers. When I sing, I start jumping. If I stand still I'm dead."

"The audience was whooping and hollering like crazy, when the song was through. That's when it really started, that night, and it's happened ever since."

—*Describing the audience's reaction to him at the Memphis Music Jamboree*

☆ ☆ ☆

"All the yelling is good because it covers up all my mistakes—if I hit a sour note."

"I've wanted to perform again in public for a long, long time. The International [Hotel] has given me a chance to play where people come from all over. I need a live audience. It was getting harder and harder for me to perform for a camera."

—*Referring to opening in Las Vegas*

Elvis was never comfortable with interviews because he was basically shy. But he was always polite and cooperative.

ELVIS ON ELVIS

ELVIS PRESLEY'S LIFE IS a story of rags to riches. His life was the American Dream come true. But Elvis was never one to take his fame and fortune for granted. He shared his wealth with others and was always grateful for every opportunity that was given him.

He was also a man with specific views about life. A religious man, Elvis never forgot where he came from and the values that were instilled in him as a young child. He carried them with him always.

Elvis was also a man with an enormous sense of humor. He didn't take himself too seriously and could easily laugh at life or himself.

His untimely death in 1977 shocked the world. But the legacy of Elvis Presley lives on in his music, films, and, of course, the words he spoke.

"I never expected to be anybody important. Maybe I'm not now, but whatever I am, whatever I will become will be what God has chosen for me. Some people can't figure out how Elvis Presley happened. I don't blame them for wondering that. Sometimes I wonder myself. . . . But no matter what I do, I don't forget about God. I feel he's watching every move I make, and in a way it's good for me. I'll never feel comfortable taking a strong drink, and I'll never feel easy smoking a cigarette. I just don't think those things are right by me. I just want to let a few people know that how I live is by doing what I think God wants me to. I want someone to understand."

"That woman was the one who had faith, she was the one who pushed me. Marion did it for me."

—*Referring to Marion Keisker of Sun Records*

"I'm tired of being me."

☆ ☆ ☆

"If I had done what today's rock 'n' rollers are doing on stage today, I'd have been put in jail."

☆ ☆ ☆

"More than anything else I want the folks back home to think right of me. Just because I managed to do a little something, I don't want anyone back home to think I got a big head."

Waiting backstage before a concert (1966)

218

"I don't feel like I'm property. I can't get it out of my head that I'm property. People tell me 'you can't do this or that,' but I don't listen to them. I do what I want. I can't change, and I won't change."

☆ ☆ ☆

"Life is more than drawing breath."

☆ ☆ ☆

"I never met anyone who learned by talking."

"I don't want to miss out on heaven due to a technicality."

—*Addressing why he wears a Christian cross,
Star of David, and a Chi*

"Animals don't hate, and we're supposed to be better than them."

"A man [is] . . . just a little boy wearing a man's body."

"Love makes crowds disappear when you're in love."

Showing off a cake one of his German fans brought by his home in Bad Nauheim

Elvis was a familiar sight around Memphis on his Harley Davidson motorcycle.

"I'd withdraw not from my fans but from myself."

☆ ☆ ☆

"I take a shower every night, whether I dance or just sing."

☆ ☆ ☆

"When I get married it'll be no secret. I'll get married in my own hometown of Memphis, and the whole town'll be there."

☆ ☆ ☆

"You can . . . love someone and be wrong for them."

"No matter what our problem might be . . . I'll never divorce Priscilla!"

☆ ☆ ☆

"I'm not a king. Christ is King. I'm just a singer."

☆ ☆ ☆

"If you hate another human being, you're hating part of yourself."

☆ ☆ ☆

"Dreams . . . tell us truths that we've got to be smart enough to interpret."

"I am and I was."

—*Commenting on being lonely*

☆ ☆ ☆

"I like it well done. I ain't ordering a pet."

—*Commenting on eating meat at dinner*

☆ ☆ ☆

"Long after I'm gone, what I did today will be heard by someone. I just want them to get the best of what I had."

"I've learned very early in life . . . without a song, the day would never end. Without a song, a man ain't got a friend. Without a song, the road would never bend, without a song. So I'll keep on singing the song."

—*To the Jaycees in the 1970s*

"Gossip is little talk for little minds."

"I've always liked challenges. I like to prove I'm better than I was yesterday. . . . There' s no fun in making a hit unless you deserve it. I believe in that, and I'm trying to live by it."

Between scenes Elvis talks to fans and gives out autographs. Note the paper towel around his collar from his makeup session. (Los Angeles)

227

Elvis's return to Las Vegas in 1969 set records for sold-out performances.

"Everyone's nuts. Some of us just see it more clearly."

☆ ☆ ☆

"People always look good in their coffins."

☆ ☆ ☆

"If your head gets too big, it'll break your neck."

☆ ☆ ☆

"I'd rather be angry than bored."

☆ ☆ ☆

"I never feel like I'm really home until I get back to Graceland."

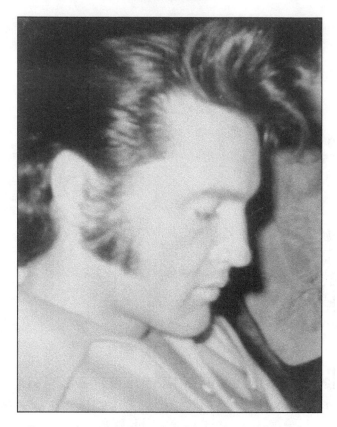

Returning from a long day at the RCA recording studios in L.A.,
Elvis pauses at the gate to his home. (1174 Hillcrest, Bel Air, 1968)

"An image is one thing, a human being is another. It's very hard to live up to an image."

☆ ☆ ☆

"I've always been a dreamer. My dreams have come true one hundred times over."

☆ ☆ ☆

"It's more important to believe in God than going to church."

☆ ☆ ☆

"God is a living presence in all of us."

"Love and warmth—that's what everyone is looking for."

☆ ☆ ☆

"Somebody once called me a sissy 'cause I was polite.
. . . There's a 'man' in manners."

☆ ☆ ☆

Press: "You're thirty-seven now. Do you disagree that
everyone over thirty is finished?"
Elvis: "I'd like to believe they're wrong."

☆ ☆ ☆

"I'm no hillbilly singer."

In 1956 Elvis knew his life was changed forever.

"I really get tired of being Elvis."

☆ ☆ ☆

"I'd rather be unconscious than miserable."

☆ ☆ ☆

"If you want to know the real truth, I don't play the guitar very well."

☆ ☆ ☆

"I can't play the guitar. I use it as a brace."

"She [Priscilla] has everything a man could want in a wife. If she's not the right girl, then there just isn't one."

☆ ☆ ☆

"If they forget me, I'll just have to do something worth remembering."

☆ ☆ ☆

"I'd like to think I've improved over the last fifteen years. But I don't want to take away from my early hits."

☆ ☆ ☆

"Life can be pretty trying when you're a hermit, even when you're a guitar-playing hermit."

"The world seems more alive at night. . . . It seems like God ain't watching."

☆ ☆ ☆

"I get lonely when I'm in one spot long."

☆ ☆ ☆

"I guess it's just something God gave me. I believe that, you know. And I'm grateful. Only I'm afraid I'll go out like a light, just like I came on."

☆ ☆ ☆

Press: "Name someone you'd rather be."
Elvis: "I can't."

236

Elvis came out nearly every night to visit his fans. Here he's holding gifts from the fans for baby Lisa Marie. (1174 Hillcrest, Bel Air, 1968)

237

"I've got everything I've dreamed of. I don't want to settle down yet."

☆ ☆ ☆

"God gave me my voice. If I ever turned my back on Him, I'd be finished."

☆ ☆ ☆

"If people just knew me. I get sick and feel bad and I get depressed, you know, just like everybody else from time to time."

☆ ☆ ☆

"I don't like sophisticated girls who pretend to be something they aren't."

"The collars keep the draft off my neck, and the capes make me feel like Superman."

☆ ☆ ☆

"I'm conscious of what I do all the time."

☆ ☆ ☆

"I believe in the Bible. I believe all the good things come from God, who is responsible for everything that happens to you. I don't believe I'd sing the way I do if God hadn't wanted me to. My voice is God's will, not mine."

☆ ☆ ☆

"I'm going to see my Momma up there [in heaven]."

"I'm not afraid to die anymore. I've seen what lies beyond, and it is far more beautiful than anything in this life."

☆ ☆ ☆

"I'm just a home boy."

☆ ☆ ☆

"It's American."
   —*When asked about his ancestry*

☆ ☆ ☆

"I like to race a speedboat because it slides around and turns like my motorcycle."

Until 1971 Elvis usually stopped to sign autographs and say hello to his fans. (1174 Hillcrest Road, Bel Air, 1968)

Press: "What happened to your slicked-down hair?"

Elvis: "I stopped using that greasy kid stuff too, just like everyone else did."

☆ ☆ ☆

"This is ridiculous! I have a mind of my own."

—*Referring to Colonel Parker*

☆ ☆ ☆

"Nobody can tell you how to live your life. I think I'm capable of life without anyone else's help."

—*Referring to Colonel Parker*

"I always felt a bit lonely when I was little. I suppose it might have been different if my brother had lived. A lot of things might have been different. But he didn't live, and I grew up alone."

☆ ☆ ☆

"It's just this little country club I run."
        —*Referring to the "Memphis Mafia"*

☆ ☆ ☆

"Look . . . I'm human."

BIBLIOGRAPHY

Dundy, Elaine. *Elvis and Gladys*. McMillan Publishing Co., 1985.

Elvis: Rock 'n Roll Legend. Susan Doll Publications International, 1994.

Elvis: A Tribute to His Life. Susan Doll Publications International, 1989.

The Elvis Years. Sterling Magazine, 1979.

The Films of Elvis Presley. Susan Doll Publications International, 1991.

Freedman, Favius. *Meet Elvis Presley*. Scholastic Book Service, 1971.

Goldmine Magazine. Kraus Publications.

Guralnick, Peter. *Last Train to Memphis*. Little Brown & Co., 1994.

Hammertree, Patsy Guy. *Elvis Presley: A Bio-Biography*. Greenwood Press, 1985.

Harbinson, W. A., and Kay Wheeler, with Ger Rijff. *Growing Up with the Memphis Flash*. Tutti Frutti Productions, 1994.

Hazen, Cindy, and Mike Freeman. *The Best of Elvis*. Memphis Exploration, 1994.

Modern Screen Presents Elvis—His Life Story. Sterling Magazine, 1979.

Modern Screen Presents Elvis—The Hollywood Years. Sterling Magazine, 1979.

Modern Screen Presents Elvis—The Romantic Years. Sterling Magazine, 1979.

Rijff, Ger. *Echoes of the Past*. Self published, 1979.

————. *Elvis the Cool King*. Tutti Frutti Productions, 1989.

————. *Fire in the Sun*. Tutti Frutti Productions, 1992.

————. *Florida Close-up*. Tutti Frutti Productions, 1987.

————. *Inside Jailhouse Rock*. Tutti Frutti Productions, 1994.

————. *The Voice of Rock 'n Roll*. Tutti Frutti Productions, 1993.

We Remember Elvis Newsletter. Priscilla Parker, editor and publisher.

Printed in the USA
CPSIA information can be obtained
at www.ICGtesting.com
JSHW051957150824
68134JS00051B/108

9 781581 823943